& Arguments &
& Negotiations &
& All That Matters &

Beadrin Pixie Youngdahl Urista

Lost Lake Folk Art
SHIPWRECKT BOOKS PUBLISHING COMPANY

Cover Photo and Design by Shipwreckt Books
Drawing by Pixie Youngdahl

© 2013, 2017 Pixie Youngdahl
All rights reserved
© 2013, 2017 Shipwreckt Books

ISBN-10: 0-9990430-0-5
ISBN-978-0-9990430-0-4
Second Printing

Arguments & Negotiations
Contents

Part One

Cancer   3

1. My Turn   5
2. Conversations with Me   9
3. My Youthful Oncologist   11
4. Post-Op Treatment   13
5. Who is a stranger to Cancer?   15
6. 1957   17
7. Stops   19
8. Back on the Planet   21
9. Hair Loss   23
10. Stretching for Optimism   25
11. Thanksgiving   27
12. Mid-December   29
13. Silent Presence   31
14. Christmas   33
15. A New Year   37
16. Back to the Clinic   39
17. Musings   41
18. Getting by with a Little Help from My Friends   43
19. Siblings   45
20. A Little Christmas Larceny   47
21. Till Death Do Us Part   51
22. For Better or Worse   53
23. Expensive by the Pound   55
24. White Flag Time   57
25. At Last   59

26. Carrying On	61
27. Spring: Myth or Promise?	63
28. On Task Again	65
29. Singin' in the Rain	67
30. Stratum	69

Part Two
Legacy Letters   71

31, Dear Grandma Alma	73
32. Dear Grandma Vera	75
33. Dear Grandpa Youngdahl	79
34. Aunt Marie Eide Tronnes	81
35. Aunt Agnes Eide Hegg	85
36. Aunt Marie Youngdahl	87
37. Uncle Jim Eide	89
38. Herve Kermit Youngdahl	91
39. Ethel Ione Eide Youngdahl Geisdorf	95
40. Herve Kermit Youngdahl Jr.	99
41. Lillian Liefgren Youngdahl	103
42. Donald Robert Anderson	105
43. Georgiann Youngdahl Anderson	107
44. Phone call	109
45. Orrin Keith Youngdahl	111

Part Three

Promise	113
Photos	121

I wish to dedicate this collection of thoughts and musings to every patient who ever allowed me to share in their fear and still found laughter to share; to every nurse, now and in the future, with learned skills, kind intentions and a sense of humor; to my friends and family, far and near, who made it clear they were not finished with me; to all my friends who are writers, Nancy Overcott, Tom Driscoll, David Fingerman and the others who encouraged me from the Minneapolis Writers Workshop. Writers are people who love words and would roll around and bathe in them. And I dedicate this to Tim, who meant it when he promised in sickness and in health; to Jason and Jodi, my kids, who can stop being afraid now, there are more chocolate chip cookies in their futures; to Elizabeth, Andy, Maren and Ellie, the best grandchildren ever, who are still young enough to hug and kiss their Nanna, even if she is bald.

Lovingly, I dedicate this book to my brother Herve Kermit Youngdahl Jr. (1937 – 2013) who taught me the value of words and ideas.

I read once a statement made by a nurse regarding her patients. If I knew the author to credit, I surely would. Instead, I will have to shamelessly borrow the thought:

The only difference between you and me, is you have a diagnosis and I do not, not yet.

Part One
Cancer

1. My Turn

Thirty plus years as a registered nurse had me interacting with cancer in its many forms. I was paid to negotiate with that wily pathology. I ran chemo on people who often suffered more with the cure than the disease, some who finessed their way through it and carried on, and others who did not.

On the brink of my retirement, it is my turn.

Cancer does not roar, it begins with a whisper. Something isn't right. Should it feel like I am sitting on something that oughtn't be there? Hardly dramatic or alarming. Perhaps I am due for a colonoscopy.

The young nurse practitioner listens attentively.

"At your age, I would worry about ovarian cancer."

Well now, wouldn't that be a foolish thing to get tangled up with?

I've done foolish things before but this was the prize.

Pelvic ultrasound, abnormal ovaries. Referral to gynecology and weeks awaiting an appointment. Let this be a sign that it's unlikely to be anything real.

Then comes the real workup. Lab work looking for elevated values on tumor markers. Repeat ultrasound and CT scan. Off to see the gyn-oncologist.

I have worked with oncologists, shared meals, cocktails and great conversation. Now I am in the patient chair. Not a cocktail to be had there, yet where better to serve them?

Information assembled, exam complete and an uncertain verdict. Labs are normal, nothing to be felt on exam, ultrasound and CT are concerning. It could be cancer, but may just be cysts or gremlins in my pelvis.

Laparoscopic hysterectomy is easy surgery. Let's do it and be rid of anything that doesn't belong there. That baby factory went out of business years ago so nothing in there will be missed.

Just prior to surgery, I am told that the doctor expects a simple procedure, in-and-out, home tomorrow, but, (there is always the but), if it is cancer, a full incision will be needed.

It's like Christmas Eve going into the OR, what will I find when I wake up??

Flash forward a few hours spent in a narcotic bliss. I am transferred to a bed in the hospital room and the pain from the full incision is my first indication that mine was not simple surgery. Loved ones are gathered at the foot of my bed, eyes like Hallmark babies looking at me. Ok, I get it.

Jen, my daughter-in-law, is half hidden behind the curtain, either waiting to bolt or to grab Jason, my son, if he tries. Jason is next, first time I've seen him speechless. He admits later that his first thought when the doctor mentioned chemotherapy was, "Shit, we'll have to duct tape her to a gurney to get her in for that!"

Jodi, my daughter, front and center also speechless but big eyed with, "I'm scared and being brave," written all over her.

Kate, a friend and nearly adopted daughter, the first and only to speak and offer the report like the professional she is, repeats precisely what the surgeon had said. Someone needed to step up, explain the situation to me, and it seems it fell to her.

Tim, on the far right, frightened and full of love, silent and watching me.

Cancer.

That's what the doctor said.

My belly hurts too much to rise up and protest the news.

I kick at the foot of the bed, well, shit-fuck. This was not my plan! Give me a minute, I'll figure it out. I need to sleep first. A hit of narcotics and I can start fresh after an escape into slumber. Those who know me well will affirm, my M.O. has always been, "Give me a minute, I'll figure this out."

When daylight comes the doctor is there to repeat what the family said in bits and fragments, or, bits and fragments are what I recall.

It is Stage II Ovarian cancer. He says I am very lucky, most ovarian cancers are not discovered until Stage III or IV, which is why it is so deadly. I was smart to go to the clinic when I did. But I do not feel especially smart or lucky just then.

The cancer was not invading other organs, lymph nodes were negative, but the surgeon washed some errant cells out and, yes, chemotherapy is indicated, sooner rather than later. Only six treatments, they say. Only.

I am *not* a patient! I take care of patients. I am professionally trained to tolerate the whining and crying.

I don't know how to do what they do.

I have never had any interest in learning how to be a patient.

Recovering from surgery didn't take long. They required that I walk in the halls and when the catheter was out the simple act of peeing would win me a ticket home. I peed for the people and walked the halls without supervision.

My nurse chased me down and said, "You aren't supposed to walk without me!" I laughed and told her she had better things to do, that she walked those halls plenty and didn't need a companion. I strolled on and told her, "Don't try to keep up with me. Just carry on!"

I won. Called Tim later and he came for me early in the morning on my second post-op day.

We got home, I sent him on his scheduled hunting trip in Canada, confident I could manage myself. Gege, my sister, insisted that she come to help me so Tim could head north knowing I was not alone.

Gege and I always enjoy time together but she is, in fact, much more frail with health problems than I was with just a gash in my belly. It became a contest to see who was tending to whom. I woke up early on about day six and felt bored and sick of feeling confined. I told her I was getting dressed and we were going to Rochester to a fabric store. She was appalled and tried to talk me out of it.

I rose from the chair and announced that I was going back to bed for a spell and hoped her attitude would improve when I got up. She rolled her eyes and looked a great deal like my mother as I stomped off to my room. When I got up again we compromised on a trip to Winona to run through Target.

Who knew going to Target would feel so liberating? The red and white hundred dollar store seems so enchanting. Cat litter in big bags, paper towels, gee gaws for an already overflowing kitchen, it's all there, calling out to me. My debit card has suffered from lack of use and is happy to see the light.

It felt like I had conquered post-op recovery and was ready for whatever they had in store for what was left in my belly. Ok then, let's do this thing!

2. Conversations with Me

Dark windy rainy Sunday.

Perfect for sewing, knitting and TV watching.

So, Pix, how ya feeling?

My bladder hurts. Not uncommon to get an infection from a catheter in the hospital. Antibiotics assault my tummy. I am learning about the delicate balance between ailments and their cures.

What do you want to journal about?

Don't know. Only know what I don't want to journal about!

No reflections on good health and life.

No inspiration, sentiment or Chicken Soup clichés. If anything interesting is to be said it will be hidden in the ordinary.

3. My Youthful Oncologist

Back in that surreal world of an oncology office, I am greeted by the perkiest adolescent practicing medicine. I suspect her mom drives her to work. She is clearly skilled and ever so competent but, really, how does a nurse with thirty years' experience take advice from someone with still flushed cheeks wearing a size eight skirt?

She makes with all the pleasantries then asks, "So, you are a nurse, you quit smoking for twenty-five years and started again. Why?" (Concerned smile.)

"Because I went to Paris for a week."

"Tsk. Well, I went to Paris for a week and I didn't start smoking."

"You weren't having enough fun. Try again!"

Goody for you, oh perfect one. You're too young to smoke anyway.

She reviewed all the meds she prescribed for side effects and I told her I had some pot I was going to try. Obviously, she has not dabbled there either. "I wish you hadn't told me that. I won't put it in your chart."

I'm not going to mention wine or she'll have me in a treatment program or put me under house arrest for being a senior delinquent. As she matures in her practice, she'll come to see that patients are whole people, not just those frightened things sitting in the chair. I hope I helped her with that lesson.

On a subsequent visit she asked "How are those cigarettes?"

"Great."

She'll learn more effective ways to frame a question, too.

When my youthful oncologist is finished with the teenage, authority-resistant Pixie, she turns me over to the nurses for a poke and five hours of therapeutic poison. Surely the cauldrons are bubbling over with my magic potion. Port-a-cath was placed yesterday and it went well. The Versed-Fentynl IV cocktails are worth the price of the procedure.

My family and loved ones are making it clear they are not finished with me yet, so I guess I must buy the package. Fact is, I'm not done with them either. I'll pull up my big girl pants and do this thing.

The room is large and plush. Huge recliner with heated seat, TV with DVD. The staff is warm, welcoming and well trained in this specialty.

Here we go. One poke into the port on my upper chest and some adjustments on the pump and the first of six rounds of poison starts coursing through my veins.

First is Prednisone and some Benadryl to ward off allergic reactions to the toxic medicine. Then the Taxol, which takes about three hours to run. This is followed by Carboplatin. At the end of the treatment, they actually drain each drop into me, though I know IV bags are always overfilled. I asked why. They reply, the stuff is too hazardous for the bio-medical waste so it's put in me instead. Doing my part to keep Minnesota green!

I am never alone, the book and the knitting I brought remain in my bag. My family hangs out and eats lunch. The staff are in and out frequently. The time does go by easily enough and I feel perfectly fine throughout. See, it's one of the tricks of the trade, fix it so they go home to be sick!

4. Post-Op Treatment

Friday

feel great! Prednisone still acting like cocaine in my system and persuading me that I must be a chemo champ! This is a breeze. I should hire out to do it for others.

Going to the Rushford Clinic for another magic potion. It's a small injection of a fancy and expensive drug to keep my blood counts, specifically white cells, from bottoming out. I can get groceries and run errands while I am in town. I can sing in my car and smile at everyone I see. Still have hair. Over the bladder infection. And healed up from the surgery. Life isn't so difficult after all. The doctor cautioned me that this injection will cause bone pain as the marrow is stimulated to work overtime. I've got Ibuprofen for that. Maybe I'll make a good dinner.

Saturday

The ooh-ahh bird sings with every movement. Did I break my hip? My femur? My thighs would be fine if the drumming with baseball bats could be stopped.

Ibuprofen, hell. I'm back to the post-op Vicodin. And soft whimpering.

Narcotics are the answer, whatever the question.

Sunday

Walking underwater. Knot in my stomach, no vomiting but I feel like I am hauling road gravel for MnDOT. I won't vomit with the Zofran on board. Can't sleep, can't pace. Couch to bed to chair to couch. Gut full of pills. One pill makes your larger, one pill makes you small.

Tuesday

Twenty percent improvement in function, anxiety up seventy-five percent. Pacing. Ativan is the fix.

Thursday

One week. This sucks. The doctor said this treatment was so easy, if I were still working, I would be punching the clock. That could only be true if my full-time job was watching *Law and Order* reruns.

If I could sleep, I could tolerate the endless, restless, fatigued days.

Yesterday I swore I wouldn't go forward but I will see how today goes. Making no promises about more.

5. Who is a stranger to Cancer?

Why?

Why do folks say, "Why me?"

"It's not fair." What is fair? Who better? We are living organisms like leaves on trees, bears and mice. All systems are subject to failure and eventual death.

Everyone is touched by disease and cancer is uncommonly ordinary. To be sure, it is more frightening than a sinus infection or cat allergy but it's all the same to a living organism. Organisms are things to be fixed, to self-heal or to overcome.

I had personal and professional experience with the challenges of this particular pathology. My family is a collective Petri dish for rogue cells to rally. My oldest brother had thyroid cancer at thirty-seven. After surgery, he has gone on without it. My sister had two separate breast cancer surgeries (good thing she had only two breasts or she may have dabbled in yet another), two rounds of chemo and she is now on to other ailments. My other brother had colon cancer last year, rough time of it but carrying on now. The youngest in the family, I waited until all their dust had settled before taking my turn.

My father died at forty-three of pancreatic cancer. He drank too much scotch and vodka so he had all the risk factors. Still, he was too young and I was only five. I remember fragments of him but many of them surround those days at the end.

6. 1957

It must have been a forced march to show-and-tell in kindergarten that would have me standing in front of anyone to say anything on any subject.

Somehow, I was standing there displaying, without narration, a new scarf. The teacher was trying to promote discussion and so, asked me, "Where did you get that pretty scarf?"

"At the hospital." (A girl of few words.)

"Why were you at the hospital?"

"To visit my daddy." (Am I finished yet? Please??)

"Oh? Is your dad sick?"

"Yes, he had Yellow Johnson and then it turned into cancer." My translation of words I'd heard from the adults around me.

I was allowed to go back to my rug at that point. Later, I missed a few days in the spring of that school year to attend his funeral.

As an adult, and a professional, I found snippets of memory and tried to hold them for him, for my mom, for my siblings, of those days.

7. Stops

The incision was an unstraight line.
Cross hatched with bloody suture.
A rolling railroad track,
leading from the onset of illness:
"My guts hurt all the damned time,
even when I'm not hung over,"
to a certain terminal end
marked with gladiolas
and organ music.
A meandering route with costly
and painful stops
in hellish places.
"After the surgical recovery
we'll try some deep radiation treatments."
Stop
pretending you'll ever be well.
"You see, sir, my husband has been ill
when he is back to work, we can catch up
on the mortgage."
Stop

believing your own lies.
"You can't take dance lessons.
I need you to take care of your sister,
and help with your dad."
Stop
being a child.
"Yes, I can work all the split shifts
my family will manage."
Stop
thinking it will get better.
"Daddy? Why did they cut you?"
Stop
believing in permanence.
A tiny finger traces the wound,
every stop,
memorizing its jagged edges,
waiting for healing
long after the earth consumed
its ragged stops.

8. Back on the Planet

A full week of recovery time and I am itching to get off the couch, into some real clothes and away from home for a spell. I never knew a trip to Winona could be so exciting. I want to drive my car too fast, play old rock and roll too loud and sing badly with each tune.

First stop, Winona Health for a slightly overdue mammogram. Can't have enough medical procedures. Perhaps I should update my immunizations and maybe schedule a colonoscopy, too!

Next stop, the yarn store to indulge in fabulous wool I had only admired before. Nothing like cancer to support my already refined rationalization skills.

By the time I get home, I confess, I am ready for some couch time and reruns of *Will and Grace*, but my attitude is greatly improved.

9. Hair Loss

This is the first thing that cancer patients stress about. It is a daily reminder that something has gone awry. We can't see the disease nor the ravages the chemo can do to kidneys and GI tract. So, we focus on the obvious. I have three wigs, all blonde, scarves of every size, shape and color, knit hats that I sewed but my favorite head covering is a White Sox baseball cap that a friend bought me on a summer day at Comiskey Park in Chicago. The Sox played the Twins that day, so I cheered for both teams.

When I am going out I use a wig or wrap one of my gorgeous scarves around my noggin. Once I leave the mirror I forget that I'm bald under there. I waltz around with an ignorant confidence and smile at everyone like I always do. I've never been met with any looks of pity, nor any offers to carry this old broad's packages for her!

The hair loss is everywhere. These are things we don't think of until the dry skin on your arms itches so bad you scratch it into bloody rows. Who thinks about nose hair?? Well, it serves a function. It filters air and helps keep nasal mucosa moist. My nostrils make for good sized air tunnels and my nose hurts from the dryness. My eyebrows have fallen out nicely. I always had this Groucho Marx unibrow thing going on and my hairdresser waxes and plucks at every visit. They have fallen out to the perfect light arch I used to pay money for.

Eyelashes, mine are short, blonde and spindly anyway, but there is enough left for a little mascara to grasp onto. I can leave the mirror thinking I look just fine.

Hairless legs and armpits are a pleasant break.

And, we can be grownups, hair is gone in those personal places too. I hadn't seen that little girl hoo-hoo since I was ten. It might be time to take up pole dancing at the Senior Center.

10. Stretching for Optimism

Some really cool things about cancer:

1) I always hated my hair, too fine and no volume despite all the expensive product cluttering my vanity. Perhaps I'll sprout great hair, thick, curly, maybe auburn.

2) Weight loss without hunger. I lost some after the surgery and now drop about six pounds after each treatment and regain three pounds before going back. It might all balance out too, my jeans are feeling better. My real size is an eight but the twelve just feels so good!

3) Won't have to shave my legs for months. Perhaps it's time for a beach vacation.

4) Getting lots of knitting done without any guilt about sitting all damn day.

5) Visits, phone calls, mail from so many good people. I get to find out what I already knew, that my life is full of high quality folks. Having always been drawn to interesting people and, shame on me, intolerant of those who bore me, I now see the final result of selectivity. The best men and women in the world are my friends.

6) I hardly have to do any Thanksgiving cooking. I will stuff the giant bird the neighbors raised for us and just enjoy the family. I could gladly pass the cooking torch onto the next generation and make it a new tradition.

Having said all that, in two more weeks, when I am hating each hour of the long, fatigued days, I will have to remind myself of all this. I know how that will go. I'll look at this list and say, "Pix, you are full of bullshit!"

But, for now . . .

Things to do while dying on the couch from chemo:

1) Watch *Intervention* while drinking wine and smoking. You can wonder if your family would be subject to similar scrutiny, write you treacly letters before sending you off to a plush treatment center and raising your kids while you are gone.

2) Watch the *Food Network* and feel brave about not wanting to eat any of that stuff.

3) Notice the commercials for hair care products and hair removal ads knowing you won't call, even if they will send two for the price of one.

4) Be glad you don't have diabetes or crippling arthritis.

5) Rejoice that this is the only time in your life nobody expects anything from you.

11. Thanksgiving

ixteen of my favorite family members arrive at my door, all bearing food and laughter. It is 60-degrees and sunny.

My four grandkids and two great nephews are wild and screeching all over our five acres.

While food is cooking, the adults gather around the shed with rock and roll music playing, beer and wine pouring and bean bag games in full swing.

Photo ops abound.

My son and daughter are a high contrast in style and personality but have forever been fast friends. To me, even now, there is no symphony in the world lovelier than the sound of my kids laughing together. Growing up, they snitched on each other, lied to cover up for each other, wished they were an only child sometimes but they sure did circle and interrogate one another's choice of spouse! It worked out, they approved after enough shared meals and beer.

Both chose wisely. Both were married 9 weeks apart. Both got into competitive baby making. All the grandkids were born within three years of each other. It's another generation of pals, sharing secrets and mischief. We did well.

My niece gifts me with some pot and a one-hitter pipe. Not the first such gift I have stashed. I now have a nice supply of recreational therapeutics on hand.

I haven't smoked any yet, but when I do, I'll blast some *Rolling Stones* and relive the Sixties like a good Baby Boomer.

If you drive by and see a sign that says Make Love Not War you will know I am feeling ok.

Now, the feast is consumed, the guests are gone, and on Tuesday I go in for labs so they can ok me for another chemo assault. How does passing a test end with a reward like that?

12. Mid-December

What better time to be sick than winter when there is nothing in particular to go outside for? It is the anniversary of my mother's death twenty-nine years ago. I light a Yahrzeit Candle for her and wonder what she would think of me, bald headed and lazy. Not much probably. She was a quiet Norwegian. She'd have patted my hand and made some coffee. Some days I could still love a cup of coffee with her and of course, some days I still fight with her. Just now, the coffee would be nice.

13. Silent Presence

 have told Gege that if she ever misses Mom to come to my house because Mom is in my bathroom mirror at six a.m. every day. Dead thirty years now, she seems to have found eternity in my bathroom. I hope she can't see herself, she was a vain thing and I have to say, she looks pretty rough some days.

We meet there and brush our teeth together. She helps me with my makeup, teaching me that make up doesn't help all that much anymore.

At bath time, she returns but averts her eyes in a gesture of modesty, a value she treasured and tried to instill.

She remains silent on the things I would finally like to know. Should this be a surprise? She said little when she had form.

Nonetheless, I inquire on those curious days.

"When you were thirty-seven and got the news that baby number four was coming, how despondent were you in the dark hours when Dad was out partying and you were overwhelmed with the first three?"

"Did you really like eating turkey necks or was that a ritual of self loathing on Thanksgiving?"

"When you didn't sleep at night but sat in the dark with the glow of your cigarette marking your presence at the table, what demons held you there?"

"Don't you think it is safe now to tell me about the cousin who was pregnant out of wedlock and 'went away' for a year? That infant would be retired by now. It is not your shame to bear."

"Those ankle strap shoes of yours that I saw in an old black and white photo. Did you dance in them? Ever? Enough?"

"When Dad died, so young, did you punish yourself for all the times you'd wished it so? Did you forgive yourself for that common wifely curse?"

"Did you ever want to bail out on the entire project?"

"Ok, so you never told secrets but if you did, with whom would you have shared them?"

"When my kids find me in their mirrors, what will they ask of me?"

She remains mute. She'll be back tomorrow, no doubt. If sainthood were mine to bestow, or I thought she desired it, I would withhold it until she 'fessed up, answered me. But then, who needs a saint looking over their personal routines?

In the week after treatment my anxiety becomes more acute than the physical misery. I am fatigued but cannot sleep. My restless legs syndrome, chronic for decades but well-handled with medication, finds a path to befriend the anxiety. They party all day at my expense. I pace. I take pills. I lie down, I get up, I pace. I wish to be put into a medical coma. Unlikely my oncologist will go for that, huh?

It passes in a week. I am so relieved that I choose not to recall it while I groove on being able to go about my regular business. Then comes the day for another treatment, my dog barks in the yard and I jump in my chair. Anxiety is moving in again.

14. Christmas

I am a Jew by choice, converted some years ago. However, we still celebrate the traditions of a cultural holiday. This is the first year in forty-one that I have not been with my kids. They are all together, with my sister's family, at my daughters. I am on the couch at home. Merry Merry and Ho Ho Ho, however it lights your candles.

Haven't we all had dreams that were oddly present? Christmas Eve I could not sleep, aching and anxious and so, so tired. Were I more inclined to crying, I'd have been wailing from frustration.

I drifted in and out and found myself back in NE Minneapolis in the home of my junior high best friend and more importantly, her dear mother, my adolescent savior, Alvina. Let me introduce you:

In seventh grade my new junior high friend, Dianne, took me to her house. Heat and the scent of cinnamon assaulted upon entering the back door. We were in Alvina's kitchen.

"Come in and sit down! You have to eat some rolls. I sure don't need them. I'm getting so heavy! I'm so glad Dianne finally brought you home, but I look a mess." She ran her hands through beauty shop hair, probably one day shy of another shampoo and set.

Beauty shop appointments, the great indulgence of the working class in the Sixties. Alvina's ever-present anxiety would grow in the forty-eight hours preceding her appointment until Dianne and I eventually took to setting her hair for her on brush rollers with harsh plastic pins that left dents in her scalp if we fixed them in place especially well.

"I bet your mother isn't heavy," she asked regularly over the years. "Don't I look too heavy?"

She punctuated the question by lifting her stomach with an inward breath, her work-weary hands pressing at its center, offering us a sideways view. No response expected. As the soft folds regained their position she reinforced them with a warm caramel bun, sticky, sweet, billowing with calories and love.

I have her recipe, written in her own hand and style, misspelled, no discernible order, composed entirely of run-on sentences, just the way she spoke. The recipe begins with, "Melt some ole in a pan," and becomes less specific after that. I've tried to follow it, to create the smell and taste and sugary mess of Alvina's caramel buns.

The result is always melancholy. I have the directions but am somehow inadequate to the task. I want to decipher the code within, "Scald milk until hot and add flour until the dough is just right."

Secrets and magic that from my oven become, well, just bread.

I grew up to be a nurse. Dianne married boring men and our lives took different paths. But Alvina, from the first bologna sandwich through all the lard fried hamburgers and eggs fried in bacon grease after sleepovers, fed me love and acceptance with a running apology for all she could not forgive in herself. Her apologies were wasted on me, I thought she was flawless.

She became a patient in the clinic where I worked and I would hold her age spotted hand when she had to have labs drawn. She always dressed up for her clinic visits and I wondered who was setting her hair.

One morning I came to work and the doctor I worked with called me to his office and closed the door. "I got called last night," he said, "Alvina died."

So there she is again on Christmas Eve. I was taking care of my grandkids, her grandkids, all the noise and madness that implies. Alvina told me, "you have to sleep now, just sleep."

I argued that I had all these kids to watch and she promised she would tend to them and would sit right there until I was good and asleep. And she did.

I slept under Alvina's simple, always tender watch. Such things are silly of course, but I'm pretty sure I felt her touch my cheek.

There are things we carry from those junior high halls. Modern math, history, first loves, and the last vestiges of innocence.

Lucky are the adolescents, discovering bad skin and finding their feet too big, their hair too fine, their clothes too ugly, to find a surrogate parent, a special teacher, that becomes as lasting as the stone and brick buildings that shelter them when they are twelve years old.

On Christmas morning, I wake up to an email with videos and photos from my family's celebration, each sending me a greeting. I watch the kids open gifts I sent them.

It makes up for the quiet evening we had. They will come down for New Year's when I will surely be in a more festive state of mind.

15. A New Year

I am like a hibernating bear. Not much to do but catch up on old movies anyway. The spring is always our reward and none better than this year, when I am healthy and hauling rocks to place around the gardens. This year I want to teach myself how to build stone walls for my climbing plants. Tim will shudder at the idea but will become engaged when I start digging and stacking. My ideas have typically morphed into his projects. I'm the idea person, he does the heavy lifting.

16. Back to the Clinic

'm fine. I'll do it. They haven't killed me yet. As I approach the end of this journey I am surprised that I have come this far. I never expected I wouldn't survive, just that I might buck and quit, like high school.

Ok, my family dragged me every time and gentled me through the recovery. Tim has become a nurse, cook, housekeeper and overall Domestic God. He has put himself at some risk however. I know now he can do laundry and make a bed!

17. Musings

Wouldn't one expect, in the wee small hours, some grand wisdom about life might arrive?

Not for me. I work through the same musings I have pondered forever when I am handling gorgeous yarn, completing a quilt project to give to a friend, writing a phrase or two that sound just right.

I have considered the nursing time I spent on the other side of this big chair. I hope I was half the nurse to my patients as I have had so far in this experience. I wish now I could thank each of my patients for the lessons they taught me, when I thought I was the learned one.

Thanks to Mercedes, ovarian cancer, whose husband told her he was sick and tired of her being sick and tired. Mercedes drove herself to and from each harsh treatment. She came in for a treatment once so sick that I took her to the hospital in my car and tucked her into bed there. No husband to be found.

Thanks to Kathy, with a breast tumor at age twenty-eight, three small boys, a now and then boyfriend and a sickly father, her only support. The boys would come with her for her treatments and dash up and down the halls of the clinic. She left this world with those three orphans having very little to hold on to.

Thanks to Clarence with his big voice, big smile and gastric cancer. He continued to hunt deer, dragging them through the woods until internal bleeding landed him in the hospital.

Thanks to the frail ones and the hearty ones. All were a blessing. I have learned this: folks with cancer have their priorities right. No complaints about elbow pain, teeth itching or splitting fingernails.

They treasure the good days, as I do. They taught me about grace and good humor. May their memories be forever blessed.

18. Getting by with a Little Help from My Friends

I have long known that my life is chock full of high quality people. And now, there is a whole parade of them calling me, emailing me, sending me gifts, bringing me gifts, visiting with me, making me laugh. That's the best part, the laughter.

I am drawn to folks who are witty and interesting. My collection of friends has developed over the years and now surrounds me, all sparkly and colorful. I was never thinking, I'd better save this or this friend for when I get cancer, but here they are.

A friend from St. Paul drove down with lunch for me, books, hand knitted socks and great conversation. The best friends one could ever find in the neighborhood have come by with homemade soup. They are comfortable visiting while I lie on the couch in my robe. My Rabbi and friends from Temple call, then come by with soup, flowers and much to discuss. Ideas make for the best conversation. My elite, i.e. small, writers group friends come by too, email, and don't mind one bit that I am bald. They inspire me to write, to let the chemo kill that internal editor and get words on a page again. My dear friend in Williamsburg, Virginia sends encouraging emails and a card after each treatment. She meets me, laden with gifts, for a treatment in mid-December. Our daughters join us and the five hours we spend together are filled with warmth and really good food.

Friends who arrived from Russia about thirty years ago make a visit to Rochester and we spend an afternoon cooking, eating and catching up. I hear from friends on *Facebook* that have been absent from my life for twenty years or more but renew all my warm memories of time we shared. Gifts of flowers and wine come by mail and Fed-Ex.

I hope never to have to return the favors under the same circumstance, but I surely will. Minus the illness, I plan to reciprocate all the love and kindness. Perhaps one huge party this summer. Stay tuned neighbors, it could get boisterous over here.

19. Siblings

fter my dad died, Mom worked split shifts as a waitress as well as helping out at the corner store across the street. My siblings took turns watching over me. Each offered a different experience.

Gege was a young teen and took me with her on dates and dragged me to church events, which she loved. Always a failed experiment.

At church, I would hide beneath tables or cling to her legs waiting to get out of that place. Going on dates was a better idea. Once, riding in a car with other teens, she told me we were in St Paul. Outrageous! Minneapolis residents have no reason to cross the river. I thought I'd been kidnapped and threatened to tell Mom.

Orrin had a different style. He would leave me alone, offering to bring back a candy bar, which he would, five minutes before mom got home.

Kerm offered adventures no other kid was able to enjoy in our working class neighborhood. He was an intellectual, or as I thought, just odd.

Fluent in German and French, in the early Sixties Kerm would take me to browse musty old book stores while he hunted for literature written in the original languages. Together, we made long visits to dark and mysterious coffee shops on the U of M campus. There would be bongo players accompanying poets reading. Kerm would buy me espresso while reading or writing.

I loved being with him. Who knows, I may have seen Bob Dylan on one of those crude stages. Kerm introduced me to jazz before rock-and-roll captured my attention, and to classical music on 33 rpm records in his apartment. My forever image of Kerm is that of a very tall, lanky man, cigarette glowing, books and yellow legal pads, his voice crooning along with Sara Vaughn on *Lullaby of Birdland*.

In the past year, Kerm's health has declined severely. While I sat at his side in the ICU, sure it would be his last visit there, to calm both our fears I asked him to sing to me. He did. It was priceless. We both survived that episode to share conversations about music, books and movies yet again.

He is in a nursing home now, but still retains that gorgeous rich baritone voice. I have often wanted to record it. I told my sister how comforting his voice is to me and she got one of her big sister expressions and replied, "It is our dad's voice." That explains it.

Gege is as concerned and attentive as she has been since the day I was born. We have never been more than a phone call from each other's reach and are still 'the first call' when anything hilarious or troublesome occurs. We raised our kids together, like barn cats. Any kid needing a hug or a scolding would receive it from the first mom at hand. It's good to keep kids confused about their parentage so more love can be passed around. She is not well either now, but still concerns herself about me. She needn't, but I can't stop her. It's her job.

My brothers, being older than Gege and I, were not so present during those busy years of family. Kerm being fourteen years older than me, and Orrin, ten years my senior, were mostly living out of town during my rebellious years when no adult in the family was eager to challenge me.

Orrin lives in Mississippi, retired from a career in the Marine Corps. Much of his life was spent far from home, including Japan, Vietnam twice and all the home years in the south.

He represents for me an entire generation of young men sent to the jungle to return home again with an eerie and too often destructive silence about the experience. There is a familiarity for most all Baby Boomers about these men. I am grateful that his scars didn't lead him in the too common path of drugs, mental illness and homelessness. I grieve for those who survived the war only to come home to a long hell.

20. A Little Christmas Larceny

For all the little sisters of that war, I offer the following anecdote:

A Marine Corps issue green duffle bag with its wrinkled and dull colored contents spread wildly around the floor announced that my brother was home on leave. Cigarette debris, already an abundant feature in the house, increased. My mother's voice took on a certain lightness. Her boy was home. To her, all his mess and chaos were as sweet as baby powder on her hands.

An aluminum foil tree with a rotating colored light gave a ballroom effect to the scene: red, yellow, blue, green, again and again. Under the tree, for the first time in his life, my brother had placed gifts for the family. Home after his first tour in Japan, he must have had a mitt full of payday cash on his way to the airport and an overwhelming moment of charity in his heart on his way home for the holiday.

At ten years of age a girl will inventory the Christmas booty daily. My package-shaking skill developed to a high level. Orrin had even wrapped the gifts, or at least he asked a friendly Japanese clerk, one no doubt enchanted by his woeful blue eyes, to wrap them.

The packages were brilliant with color and shine despite their long journey home, boxer shorts and tee shirts pressed all round them.

There was a red one for Mom. For Gege, a square box wrapped in a riot of pine trees on gold background. Just a gesture at shaking stirred a musical response from within.

For Kerm and his wife, a gift wrapped in foil that reflected the primary colors from the spinning light above.

But there was no package for me.

I was not without hope. I looked around and through the packages over and over. I decided it must be an error. I went to Orrin's room and found him smoking a cigarette and listening to county music on a small, black transistor radio. I flat out asked him why my gift was not under the tree. He turned down the radio to accept my query then turned it back up and said, "Why would I get you anything?"

It was clear a new approach was called for. "Did you get me a puppy? Is that why it isn't under the tree?"

"No, I told you. I'm not getting you anything."

In the days leading up to Christmas Eve, I checked regularly for the gift, sure he was teasing me. He would watch me crawl about on my knees with my skinny behind in the air, rearranging and counting packages. The ones that were there held little interest for me anymore. I needed the one that was not there.

"If it's not a puppy, is it a kitten? Did you get me a bike?"

He held his ground, smoked the cigarettes he'd purchased at discount on the military base and brought home in cases for the family. He listened to that little black radio, the technological miracle of the early sixties.

Christmas Eve arrived and I generously gave him yet another chance to slip a bit of magic under the tree. It didn't happen.

Before we sat down to dinner I made a bold move. "If you forgot to shop for me, can I have the radio you brought home?"

"No, you can't. So there, Merry Christmas."

I knew the Marine Corps had cost him some pounds and that his posture was different now, but despite the stubbornness about this gift, he showed no evidence that Corps made him mean. Since he was home, he'd taken me for a malted at the corner dairy store and teased and smiled at me just like before.

It was Christmas though. Mom was beaming as she brought bowls and platters to the table. And I decided I was mad.

I went to his room and found the little black radio. I turned it on quietly and rolled the dial on the side to find a rock and roll station. I wasn't listening to country music for the rest of my life! I shut it off and carried it to my room. The small bedside stand had a drawer for all my valuable treasures, shiny rocks and hair clips mostly. I pulled the drawer out and slipped the radio behind it, replaced the drawer just slightly ajar to accommodate the stash behind.

A smug and satisfied little girl presented herself at that holiday table and smiled sweetly at the soldier brother across from her.

Aunts and uncles and neighbors and friends filled the evening. My brother went upstairs from time to time and became more irritable as the evening wore on. It was late when we settled to open the gifts and I was allowed to distribute them, knowing each and every one from my days of counting and stacking.

Orrin stood by the space heater and accepted thanks and praise from everyone for the gifts he had chosen. Perfume for Mom. An electric percolator for Kerm and Lil. A lacquered jewelry box with a dancing ballerina for Gege. Being the youngest there was no shortage of little girl gifts for me to open and in the litter of paper and ribbon I almost forgot about the gift I didn't get and the Grinch-like action I had taken.

Orrin stood in a sullen posture. As I swept past him with a new game to set up he grumbled, "Hey, if you ever find that transistor radio, it was supposed to be your Christmas gift."

Not old enough to steal and lie at the same time, I threw my arms around his neck in the hug I had been so wanting to give him and squealed, "I know where it is!"

I ran up to my hidey hole and returned with the radio to show the family. It played only rock and roll tunes ever after.

Now my brothers both call before every treatment and a week later to follow up. Perhaps we all see that there will not always be the four Youngdahl kids, and it seems things could change sooner rather than later. Every phone call now ends with, "I love you." Words rarely heard from big brothers before our Golden Years. It means a great deal to me to hear their voices.

The value of the people who have known us forever cannot be underestimated. My siblings are an odd collection of style and personality but they are mine, beginning to end.

21. Till Death Do Us Part

ow can those dewy-eyed brides and grooms know what they are promising? They just want to clutch one another until forever. None of us knows of forever.

Neither Tim nor I have suffered great illness. Through flu (always introduced from our school age kids, little vectors) and back pain, colds, minor surgeries, burns, lacerations and bouts of melancholy, we sympathize and roll our eyes as life mates will do.

Tim is frightened of all things medical. He would rather build a wing on a hospital single handed than sit in a surgery waiting room. I had hoped to never put him in that place. He was fortunate to become a father when maternity wards had a fathers lounge where anxious men hung out smoking and watching television, waiting for news from the nursing staff. Had he been in the delivery room, the staff would have had trauma to deal with when he hit the floor in a dead faint.

Now he is a caregiver. I see fear in him, as a spouse will, but his actions deny anything but competence and love.

Housework, cooking, errands, tending to the chickens, grocery shopping and periodic kisses on my forehead are his life pattern for now.

We could have simplified things by transferring my care and treatments to Mayo, Rochester being only forty-five miles from current home. But Minneapolis is my home town, and the care I was offered there assured me that all was well. Tim did not hesitate to dismiss any inconvenience in driving one hundred-fifty miles every three weeks.

One treatment day, the roads were snow and ice covered. I threatened to cancel. He wouldn't hear of it. We took his truck. He'd have dragged me on a sled behind a snowmobile if necessary.

He rubs my bald head and smiles. Can he still see the same girl he met in seventh grade?

I have a modest annuity accrued from my working years. I offered him a trip to Africa hunting as a reward. He said, "You don't have to do that."

It's not near enough.

22. For Better or Worse

re you still here?
You were sure to leave me
when the work headed west
or north, or east.
I was only keeping you until then.
After the wedding, when you realized
how long until forever,
you were just too shy to ask me to leave.
I was willing to save you that
but lacked the courage
to ask for travel money,
so I stayed.
During the high-speed years, raising kids,
who had time to look across a room
and contemplate the other adult there?
It's a small team,
you and you
against them.

Certainly the dark hours of quiet
when the kids were crashing through the world
like they were the first to discover it.
We both wondered.
But then, bigger questions entered the mix,
LIFE, DEATH, GOD, PENSIONS.
And now, after all these years,
I want to settle in.
You seem to want me here.
You are finally laughing at my jokes.
Your voice on the phone, midday,
is a soothing surprise to me.
Soon, we'll have to admit
this thing is getting serious.

23. Expensive by the Pound

am told the little subcutaneous injection I receive the day after treatment to keep my white cells adequate to fight off ordinary infections costs about $5,000 each.

For that, it should make me immune to malaria, snake bite and Bubonic Plague. That is just the little shot to minimize the ravages of the main course.

Lucky me, I married a man who was obsessed with security since he was bagging groceries in high school. However, does that make my health and life more valuable than all those millions who work for poor wages and no benefits?

I think not. What treatment would have been offered had I no insurance? Likely, I'd not have presented to the clinic with subtle symptoms and would have landed in an emergency room when I was riddled with misery. Easy then, nothing to be done.

So I am now a Million Dollar Baby. My dad called my sister his Million Dollar Baby and called me his Two Million. (Can we back up to some of my sister's neurosis and insecurity? Another time perhaps.) I'd be proud to tell him he was a prophet. Not sure this was what he had in mind.

To deal with all the small and large inconveniences of this illness and to be destroyed by the bills as well is beyond my ability. People do it every day. I have no answers and clearly our politicians are inadequate to the task.

This I know, the professionals who provide the care do not drive the problem. They suffer it as well. Mostly they just want to do the jobs they were trained to do. All the advances in medicine let them offer more, but at the end of the day, they do what they have always done with the tools available. They look at the profiteers with the same incredulous expression the rest of us do. Then they carry on.

My surgeon was experienced and compassionate. He had great equipment to utilize, but the expensive equipment would stand mute and hopeless without his skill.

The nurses have electronics galore to aid in their assessments, but they do not replace nursing judgment and instinct to anticipate problems. No electronic miracle can replace laughter as medicine or a gentle voice at the bedside.

Where does all the money go? Big-pharma, medical suppliers, for-profit insurance companies, marketing, and of course, the machine that goes cha-ching.

24. White Flag Time

*I*n the lobby of the Cancer Center gather aged people pushed in wheelchairs by loving daughters, sons or equally ancient spouses. I sit there hoping my scarf wrap is still straight on my head and ponder. How do they tolerate this? Is it their choice to fight the fight or is it the well intended but maybe misplaced concern about family?

Chemotherapy is still fairly crude. It means to target those cells with the black hats but wipes out useful white hat cells as well. If my vital organs were already compromised by age and other pesky chronic illness, I'm not sure I would risk them.

Sometimes we need to ask, "What am I buying?" It's a unique feature of health care. We buy without asking about the price or value. If I bought a car, (the cost of my care could surely have put a shiny new one in the garage!) I would know the price and what to expect. We don't buy clothing without cost and value comparison. If at this time, I was told that treatment might or might not be successful, more information would be in order.

There are thinking people who have a fierce belief in preserving life at all costs. I am not one of those. Whether it is my front row seat to disease and end of life as a nurse or simply my Norwegian practicality, I want value. I have a living will with narrative remarks around all the margins. The bottom line is, when I cannot engage in meaningful conversation, laugh and interact with others, stop the parade and bring in the clowns.

25. At Last

The final treatment FEELS right for a party. The course of each one followed the same routine, only the misery and anxiety perhaps lasted a day or so longer each time, or perhaps my patience became diminished, so it felt longer.

Little Dr. Perky comes in prior to the nurses to congratulate me and talk about follow up schedules. Follow up on what? The parts that were bad are all gone, my tumor markers were always normal, there should be nothing to scan, x-ray or draw labs for. I want this behind me and resist the idea of carrying on a relationship with the whole ordeal.

But, I am an obedient patient and schedule an appointment in three months.

I just want to grow hair now.

Tim and Jodi and I go to lunch at *Jax* in northeast Minneapolis when my treatment is finally over. *Jax* has long been our family's favorite celebration restaurant, and the end of chemo sure feels like something to celebrate.

One week later, the port comes out. I am appliance free.

Cancer looks better in the rearview mirror.

26. Carrying On

It has been three weeks and one day since my last dose of toxic waste. Where is my hair, huh? I accepted losing it with some patience and good humor, but now that I am done, shouldn't hair follicles respond? Come on! Its winter and my head is cold!

I am volunteering three days a week and feeling alive and full of capability. Why is my hair lazy?

My kids and grandkids are coming tonight. I have missed them. I want show them that Nanna does not have to lie about on the couch forever. Maren had a birthday. I am making chocolate cake with chocolate frosting, as she requested. By the way, this is not a box cake, flour sugar and all the rest mixed from my stash in the cabinets.

I will grow hair and not be such a concern to them again sometime soon.

27. Spring: Myth or Promise?

I've done sixty plus Minnesota winters and experience tells me, they always go away. Now, in this post St. Paddy's day snow and ice, I will go on faith.

Spring will arrive and I will examine every plant for signs of life.

I will speak gently, coax and make promises about weeding and watering that I'm not sure I'll keep.

My plants know me, they have good fertile ground, sixty feet of buffalo crap to nestle through, and an adoring but lazy gardener to praise their beauty. They forgive me for my neglect and live for my worship.

I intend to be hauling rock from the creek bed to frame them and hope to try my hand at building a stone wall. Tim winces when I suggest such projects because forty years has taught him that my ideas are his labor. Won't a little stone wall be cool though? Sure it will.

I'll sit on the patio he built, with the metal trellis around and overhead, also his design and handiwork, sipping wine and singing to the grape vines. Maybe I can take up wine making as well. What are Minnesotans if not ever-hopeful as spring draws near?

Summer will bring evening fires with rock and roll music blasting from the stereo in the shed, fireworks while the kids chase fireflies, friends and family chatting until well after dark.

These things are promised by the calendar, if not by the current weather conditions. I will be here to realize all of them.

28. On Task Again

My sick days are over, blessedly. I had my four grandkids here for spring break when an early morning call came that Gege was in the ICU after falling at home from weakness exacerbated by vomiting and diarrhea. Wait, it gets better. Her daughter, my niece Jen, had a hip replacement at the tender age of forty-one and was staying with Gege for her recovery when the 911 call needed to be made.

I ran from the house and dashed to the Twin Cities to tend to Jen's post-op needs before heading to the hospital where specialists galore prodded Gege for a diagnosis. They had several theories, none definitive. Bottom line, Gege is a train wreck and each crisis adds another bead to her string of ailments that cannot be fixed.

Just after I remarked, "Being the youngest child was cool until all the older children started to crash and burn," the call came that Kerm had passed away at the nursing home. His death was no surprise. He has been ill for a few years with no magic in sight. Still, he is gone.

I will so miss his voice on the phone. I will miss our conversations about music, movies and politics. I am grateful that we spoke just two days before his death when he called to suggest a movie on *Turner Classics* that evening. Most importantly, our conversation ended with me saying, "I love you," and his response, "I love you too, little sis." His voice, always soothing to me, was my father's voice.

His memory will be always, a blessing to me.

29. *Singin' in the Rain*

If I could sing or dance, I'd be out there with Gene Kelly and Donald O'Connor, singing, "Good Mornin', good mornin'!" However, I'd surely fracture something in the effort.

When I sing in my car I have perfect pitch and can wail with the best of 'em, Bonnie Raitt, Carole King, Elvis. I lose that skill, however, when I leave the car so it doesn't hold much promise for my future.

If I could paint, I would have a canvas as big as the side of a barn and oil paints, all bold colors. Sadly, my stick people are the peak of my art career.

I will write, as I always have. Writers observe. Writers notice gestures, a lone wrinkle on a shirt, speech patterns, facial expressions and anything that does not fit exactly. Writers love words. To a writer, words have taste and smell and texture.

Writers write to see what they are thinking. They collect images and faces, assemble them into a whole with pen and paper. The words writers choose and utilize, the ideas they express, are often a surprise to them until they read a phrase or paragraph from their own hand and find clarity.

Sometimes writers don't write. So they writhe around in pain instead. I have written more about not being able to write than any other topic. There are poems to be written, but I don't know the words yet.

Writers notice things, even things that don't belong. I noticed, went to the doctor. Noticing has made all the difference.

30. Stratum

It is imperative to go,
sometime
where the earth curves
to know,
it doesn't end at 5 p.m.
or the county line
or September 11.
Follow that edge
the prairie
the sea.
Seek the line
where the sky curtains down
and makes promises
or tells lies
to its horizontal mate.

We all look at that horizon and create a fiction about its meaning. Reaching the horizon just means moving forward to the next.

We are all in the business of following horizons. Meet yours, I will meet mine.

Part Two
Legacy Letters

To the folks who came before
Contributed to me
Paved the path for those in the future
For better
Or worse
As I recall them or the stories they left behind

31. Dear Grandma Alma

Alma Hallum Eide died and was buried in Fillmore County, Minnesota in 1932

There you were, on the empty prairie of North Dakota with 9 kids when your husband up and died for no apparent reason. Kids were quarantined for small pox at the time (1917) so the coffin was carried by the house on a horse drawn carriage for the children to see from the windows. Somehow, I imagine you watching, then wiping your hands on an apron and saying "I've got bread dough rising."

I can't know anything like that about you. Your youngest daughter, my mom, never spoke of you. What does that mean? I never questioned it as a kid, what kid ever considers their mom having a mom? Now, I wonder what she felt about you, if you ever had time to know much about her.

I know something of the Norwegian temperament, can well imagine you had little time or taste for warmth and affection. Not to worry, your daughters held together with a warmth they perhaps invented within their own hearts.

I've seen your grave up here at Highland Cemetery and tried to conjure you in my mind. I'm quite sure you would not have approved of me. Who knows? I'm sure your life was difficult and you could not know that you were something of a pioneer. Here we are now, less than ten miles apart, only my mother between us as a connection. Would I have liked you? You me?

Ole Olson Eide and Alma Hallum on their wedding day, c. 1900

32. Dear Grandma Vera
(Vera Schwerin Youngdahl died and was buried in Minneapolis on Halloween 1985)

You, I remember well. Know what, I really tried to like you, felt like I should love you. The challenge was daunting.

I get it. You had three kids, my father the eldest and most beloved. While in the hospital for the birth of your third, your husband, Alfred Youngdahl, packed up and left you. Wow. See, in the current time, people think such behavior is new. I bet this happened ever since the start of time. I could have admired your willingness to take charge of your life and your kids. You worked in Northrup King Seed factory every day. Took over that giant duplex on 4th Street NE to tend to your blind mother, had family living up and down for decades.

But, you were so bitter. You had a talent for making everyone suspicious of each other while keeping them all tied to your sphere of influence.

You outlived all of your kids. I don't even want to imagine such horror and pain. You wore it, though, like a steel cage.

This needs to be said: When my mother attempted suicide, due to her own internal pain, you came marching in to shake a finger at me, saying it was my fault for leaving her home alone too much. Shame on you. I was 14 years old and mom's depression was not of my making. The irony is, it wasn't out of concern for her, you were one of the burdens of her life, it was just an opportunity to spread around more misery. Maybe it didn't occur to you, that a 14-year-old girl, finding her mother non-responsive from alcohol and barbiturate ingestion, might be in some pain, too. Fortunately, it was not my nature, then or now, to accept blame or shame for that event.

Being a grandmother should be an honor. I see it as such. Maybe my grandkids are more loveable than the orphans you were left to deal with.

Life could have been sweeter for you, I understand. I'm not sure whose assigned task it was to make it that way. I am sorry for all your losses.

You showed me a news article about a relative of yours that died in Spandau Prison, having been charged as Hitler's finance secretary. You were proud to have a celebrity in the family tree. Really? It turns out, he was a banker of some sort and many such folks were conscripted for the Nazi party, he was one of those. You might have done better to take pride in having had a banker in the family.

We needn't go into how I had to sue your estate for photos of my dad and my family.

I suppose we all do the best we can with what is available to us. What you had in abundance was bitterness and you spread it all over the family.

I was supposed to love you and I tried.

Grandma Vera, Herve Kermit Youngdahl, Great Grandma Hulda Wilhemena Paula Schwerinn and Herve Kermit Youngdahl, Jr.
No beauty Contest

33. Dear Grandpa Youngdahl
(Alfred John Carlson Youngdahl Youngdale)

 wish I could hear your story, complete with the Swedish brogue. I know you were a street car driver in Minneapolis. I can't quite fathom how Vera swept you off your feet but it seems she charmed you long enough to marry her and father three children (Herve, Marvel and Norris) Thank you for my father.

I also know that you bailed out on that project and moved to Detroit, changed your name to Youngdale and started a whole new family. Know what? I can't blame you. I only wish I had met you.

My mom told me the story of a time when my dad traveled to Detroit for a sales convention or something and he looked you up. She said he called in the wee hours of morning so she could say hello to you on the phone. What she remembered was your heavy Swedish accent, and that you were both mighty drunk. How was it, I wonder, for the two of you to meet again? I'm sure it was one of those male bonding moments, fueled by Scotch and bravado and not one word that was meaningful but it probably meant a great deal to him. I applaud his courage, to make the connection.

If you did not know, he was alcoholic and died at age 43. We can assume he was a wounded pup. Being the oldest, he was likely the only one who remembered you at all. Perhaps his abandonment issues shaped him.

In recent times, your Youngdahl family made contact with your Youngdale family and they were gobsmacked to discover that you had this whole tribe back in Minneapolis. Your youngest grandson, Jason Youngdale, is on Face Book (I won't try to explain all that to you) and we have had some conversations. He posted a photo of you with your new family and it all looks so normal, so 1950's. You had your arms around two little girls, daughters, I suppose. I tried to figure you out in that photo. Hmm, my Grandpa. Imagine that.

For just one moment, I would like to have been one of those little girls in the photo with your protective arm around me.

I truly understand your fleeing from that life, I do. Still, having a grandpa would have been nice. I hope your second life was rewarding for you but you did leave rather a hot mess behind.

34. Aunt Marie Eide Tronnes

You were the absolute Norwegian. I never recognized the depth of your accent because it was normal to my ears. Later in life, taking care of old Norwegian women, I would be drawn to memories of you when I would hear them speak.

You became the family Matriarch whether it was your intention or not. Being one of the "older" girls, marrying that nice Canadian Norwegian (Uncle Ed Tronnes) and moving to the Twin Cities, you opened the borders for your younger sibs to follow. Your maternal role never diminished. My mother and Agnes feared and respected you like cocker spaniel pups. That fear and respect carried over to the next generation. As a small child, I can remember an event where you and the other aunts, uncles and cousins were coming to our house. My mom was fussing over food to serve and tidying up the house and she warned me, "Do not throw away bread crusts when Marie is here, she thinks that's wasteful!" Mom was not about to get scolded because her kids were fools.

You and Uncle Ed bought a tiny log cabin on Big Sandy Lake in the 1930's for about $150. It had an outhouse and a pitcher pump. Somehow, you recreated the story of loaves and fishes on summer weekends when the entire extended family would descend upon you. I think that small refrigerator must have had a walk in cooler behind it to supply all the meals you created there! Before I was born you added a bedroom, just large enough for a double bed and a small dresser.

There were two fold-out couches in the living room that met, end to end, when they were opened and there was a roll away bed in the dining area. Between two trees outside swung a covered hammock. I suspect the drunkest uncle spent the nights out there. We fished with Uncle Ed, who knew every bay on that large lake. On the end of that rickety dock sat two steel chairs with holders on the end of the dock for your fishing poles. The primary crop from around that dock was bullheads. I was horrified of those monsters but you would grind them up, bread the meat and fry it up- we called those treat "fish balls". When the rain would pound down on that steel roof, the cards came out. You taught us how to play canasta as soon as we could count by fives. I've taught the game to my grandkids and they love it as much as I did. The men stood around the wood shed, where the fishing gear and boat motors were stored, to pass around the "hidden" bottles of whiskey and beer. The aunts pretended they didn't know but the kids all did. At bedtime, you placed empty coffee cans next to the beds, no girls went to the outhouse after dark. Bears, ya know. During the night, we would hear the gentle tinkle, tinkle in the cans and in the morning, you would graciously empty them while coffee brewed. How did you do it? Boiling water on the stove to feed such crowds? You did it with perfect calm.

In 1967, you lost your beloved youngest daughter, Myrna, to a tragic shooting. I guess it was ruled suicide though the legend remains that her schmuck of a husband shot her. When, 20+ years later, her daughter appeared at your door, the image of her mother, it was the makings of a Hallmark movie. Lord, you were strong!

I don't cry much, it's a Norwegian thing, but at your funeral I fell apart when that granddaughter came through the door.

When I converted to Judaism and chose a Hebrew name, I chose Miriam to honor you and my dear Aunt Marie Youngdahl. I wish I could have done more in your memory.

Marie　　　　　Agnes　　　　　Ethel

"She said what?"

35. Aunt Agnes Eide Hegg

You and mom were only a year or so apart in age and were nearly interchangeable to a tot. You were warm and sweet, like my mom, and too passive to demand more than you got from life.

I'll always see you, sitting in your corner of the living room, crocheting doilies and drinking coffee while you and my mom watched "your stories" together. Like mom, you married an alcoholic and settled for the little security he offered. You raised three kids with love while you probably trembled with concern. You died two weeks after Uncle Kenny, I might have wished for a little more peaceful time for you but perhaps that life was all you knew. Your death was just months after Mom's. If I believed in the myths of life after and all that, you and Mom would be sipping coffee together, worrying over kids and less than ideal husbands together, knowing now that it all works out one way or another.

Here is a silly secret: You and mom looked so much alike, tiny frame, never an extra ounce anywhere. However, Mom was vain and confident that she was the prettier one. When people would remark about how much I looked like her she would always correct them, "No, she looks more like Agnes." That is fine, I am happy to look like you.

Gege and I came to visit you after we picked up Mom's ashes to sprinkle. It was the last week of your life and you sat in your chair, baby blue robe and a pink bow in your hair. What a sweet image for me to hold.

Mom (Ethel) and Agnes c. 1932

36. Aunt Marie Youngdahl

You were always the single bright light in the world of Youngdahls. Platinum blonde, ever smiling, rich laugh and only the kindest words.

You were married to my uncle Norris (Dad's youngest brother) or I'd never have been able to claim you as my own. What a gift you were to us.

It was long after our childhoods that we connected as adults and learned that Uncle Norris was a dark alcoholic, that you held that family together with pure love and wit.

You were an alonon devotee and I often quote your Marie ism's..

Listen to you, "shoulding" all over yourself.

You know, your head hears what your mouth says.

I will ever admire your courage, the day of Grandma Youngdahl's funeral- she was never good to you- none of her kid in laws met her standards. You, Gege and I walked into the funeral home with mixed feelings about the entire life shared with Vera. There were two tiny old women sitting on a couch as we walked past and one whispered to the other "Hmmph, she sure has family now, doesn't she?" You paused, turned and went to them. With a warm smile you reached out your hand and said, "I don't believe we have met. I am Marie, Vera's daughter in law, and you are?"" They smiled as if they hadn't just insulted us all and offered their names. You kneeled in front of them and took their hands, "I'm glad you were Vera's friends and could be in her life but I have to ask that you not judge her family, there is a long history within this room that you are probably unfamiliar with. Thank you for coming."

They were silenced by your grace as you rose and walked away. I told you later in the day how impressed I was at your assertive approach. You told me, "I did that for me. Had I not, I would have been angry about their remarks and that anger would never be a good thing." Wow!

After Norris died, you fell in love with his best friend, whose wife had died. You married and celebrated being together every precious day. He died a few years later and your heart was broken. Still, again, at about 80 years of age, you met a man who, of course, adored you. You took care of him at the end of his life. I so loved your belief in love. I treasure having been the recipient of that love.

37. Uncle Jim Eide

I had uncles that were fun and kind but you were the best of the best. You were only a few years older than my mom and after your dad died and left Grandma Alma on a dirt farm in North Dakota, you may have decided farming was the way to go. Or, when you were 13 or 14 she wanted one less mouth to feed but either way, you moved to Whalen, Minnesota to be raised and trained by your uncles, Helmer and Lawrence Hallum. You were the stereotypical Norwegian farmer in a community with little diversity.

You bought a farm in Newberg, you milked cows, raised crops and offered lessons in nature to a city kid. Each summer, we would take the long ride down here from the city- it was about 4 hours or more at that time because I-90 was nonexistent and Highway 52, after the airport probably, was two slow lanes. I loved coming to visit you. You had a ready smile and were quick to laugh.

Getting out of the car at your farm yard, my mom would draw a deep breath and remark about fresh air. I smelled manure but I like the smell of bus fumes. The Hallum family reunion was, and still is, held annually in Lanesboro so that was when we would likely come here. One year, the entire clan of aunts, uncles and cousins were gathered around your kitchen table drinking coffee (and sounding like Norsks!) when I came in from the yard and asked if I could pick up one of the chickens running around the barn. I should have seen the twinkle in your eye when you handed me the salt shaker from the table and instructed me, "Just shake some alt on their tails and they'll stand still and let you hold them." Why would I doubt you? So, I chased those poor hens all over the barnyard shaking salt until there was none left. Guess, what, that doesn't really work! The family was watching out the window and having a grand time. Just so you know, I've raised some chickens in recent years and told them that story. They found it amusing.

You were tender and funny. You rarely were able to leave the farm to come to Mpls, farming is an every-damn-day deal, but when you did your sisters were waiting eagerly for the fresh eggs you brought and for colored margarine. They called it "Olie" For a historical touch I'll explain this: The dairy farmers resisted colored margarine in Minnesota because, they were in the butter business, after all. In the 50's, margarine was sold in a soft plastic pack, white as lard. There was a small plastic button with yellow/red food coloring in there and after the purchase you would pop that button and work the color through the margarine. Iowa sold colored margarine so when you came up you would bring a case for the sisters.

Besides the booty you brought, my mom, Agnes and Marie were thrilled to have you visit because they adored their brothers and were ever protective. Trust me, I listened to those gals gossip and sisters in law were fair game but their brothers were Rock Stars.

I agree, especially you.

38. Herve Kermit Youngdahl
December 1913—1957

ad, perhaps I should still call you Daddy, which is where our conversation left off. Kerm and Orrin only referred to you as "the old man"

I've wondered who you were my entire lifetime. I have a few tender memories and a head full of stories told by others.

You were 43 when you died of pancreatic cancer, far too young to be able to amend your ways. Alcohol, cigarettes and a lust for living large defined your short time with us.

Things I know are true because they are my memories to keep: Feeling so safe and secure on your lap in the green rocker, feeling your voice in your chest when you spoke. You, making the "x" in my name when I was learning to write it down. You, buying me Nut Goodie bars at the store. Feeling so proud of how handsome you were when you came into my Sunday school class to pick me up because we were going to Grandma's. You wore a fedora hat and a suit. I remember you being sick. After your surgery, you on the couch in pajamas and I asked to see your incision. It was huge. I traced it and asked, "Why did they hurt you, daddy?" The day you died, mom couldn't manage you anymore, you were so weak. The ambulance came and took you to a nursing home. Mon went over to spend the day and in the afternoon Margaret and Edwin took me along to pick her up. Rules were broken to allow me in to see you and I clung to Margaret, didn't recognize you.

She nudged me toward you and said "Go see your daddy." You held out your arms and called me Schnooks. I knew your embrace and asked when you could come home. "I'm really sick." That was it. You died later that evening while Gege and I were at dance class. You should know, Mom cried, no small deal.

I know the legends as well. You drank far too much and it scarred the family and your reputation. Grandma Youngdahl was always in your corner, mothers are like that, so she made a saint of you while everyone else stayed pretty silent. The family circled the wagons around me, they weren't critical of you in my presence. Only a few years ago on my birthday I asked each of my siblings to offer me the gift of sharing a good memory about you. They'd rather have pitched in on a new car. However, true to me and my bossy ways, they each pondered a moment to fulfill my wishes. I'm not sure I even recall their responses only that I needed to hear them.

Mom was certainly in love with your charm and promises of a life much different than what she ended up with. You left too soon, or maybe not, but her life never improved.

I dream of you, those dreams are so vivid and intense. I dream of hearing your voice, struggling to hear your voice, to get you to recognize me in a crowd. I loved hearing Kerm's voice on the phone, that deep, sure baritone. I told Gege that once and she said, "Well, ya, it's dad's voice." So, I was left with that.

There is little point in wondering how it would have been, life moves at its own pace. I'm not a believer in heaven and all that but if when my life energy transitions to its next form, if my brain creates some illusion of familiarity as it flickers out, I would wish it to be you in a fedora hat, reaching out for your Schnooks.

Gege, Orrin, Ethel, Pixie, Herve   Christams 1956

39. Ethel Ione Eide Youngdahl Geisdorf
Mom: May 7, 1914—December 13, 1983

You accrued more names than fortune in your 69 years, didn't you? I wonder which of those personas served you best.

A lovely, lithe young thing, you left that empty North Dakota prairie as soon as you were able to pack that bit of luggage that I still cherish. Your photos and treasures have been safe with me. You headed to Minneapolis, by train probably, and like your siblings, moved in with your sister Marie. What sort of plans and dreams did you have?

I know you worked for at least a short time as housekeeper and nanny for a Jewish family. You said it was the only time you weighed over 100# because it was better food than you'd ever had access to!

You met dad through on a blind date, arranged by your sister Agnes (your best friend and confidante for both of your lives) and dad's aunt Ruth. They worked together in some factory or something and one of them must have said, "I have a good idea!" I'm certain you dazzled each other in short time. He knew arm candy when he saw it and must have been drawn to that sweet, sometimes devilish smile. You were married in April of 1936 and told me you went camping for your honeymoon. That may have been your first clue and you could have hidden behind a tree until he left, but...

You moved into Grandma Youngdahl's house, per the requirements of that family. You were there for 10 years, had the first three kids living in that family filled duplex. Yikes. I'm not sure how you got pregnant three times, sleeping in a bedroom with an archway to the dining room where Grandma and aunt Marvel slept. Quietly, I suppose.

In those old photos, I can see the shift, from the young flirty gal you had been, to the uncertain mother of three you had become. In about 1947 Dad had a work opportunity for a company in Denver and you were released from that grey house of Grandma's. You told me once it felt like you had been let out of jail. We have old movies of you and Gege, a toddler then, enjoying a summer day in Colorado. Your beauty and grace are captured there. I'm glad for that time.

I suppose Dad couldn't be away from his mom for long so you returned to Minneapolis, moved into the house that Grandma chose and there you were for a long 16-18 years. That was our home, the place I still dream of struggling to reach by bus or on foot, to check on you.

This is where our story began. I was number four, you were 37 years old and beleaguered by life in general. Still, you were ever loving and patient. I couldn't know how difficult your situation was, you were my constant.

Fast forward, dad died in 1957, there was no money, nothing. Kerm had mental health issues, he left home and married Lil in about 1959 or so, Orrin enlisted in the Marine Corp right after his high school graduation in 1960, Gege fell in love with Don and married him in 1962, when she was just 17. So, there we were.

You worked as a waitress and at the store across the street. There was a small widow's benefit from Social Security. Kids don't know if they're poor, your wallet was always loaded with change so it looked like security to me. You resisted aid but we needed it. One Christmas the minster from our church came with a basket full of food and wrapped gifts for us and you thanked him kindly but told him to give those to someone who needed them. There were periodically packages of government cheese and butter that you likely resented.

When did we fall apart? I wish now, that we could talk about your untreated depression and the struggle it was for you to put one foot in front of the other to walk down Monroe Street to work and carry home groceries day after day. Kids don't see things that are now obvious to me. You were worn down, exhausted by life, with miles to go.

I never, ever, for a moment, stopped loving you and I know you loved me even when you were dark and empty inside your own head.

It tumbled and rolled, all downhill. You self-medicated your crushing depression with alcohol and isolation- wrong combination. The weekends when I would come home and find you with bloody dishtowels scattered about, bleeding lacerations on your scalp from falling, I would hear you vomiting in your bedroom and pull my pillow over my head to block the sounds of your despair. You lost the house to foreclosure and we moved to an upper duplex on the north side. Still, you were a constant loving presence to me.

Maybe had you raised a fist to the skies and let your anger outward instead of letting it consume you internally, however, that was not your nature.

You saw me rebelling, it was clear I would drop out of school and leave you, one way or another. You did make a decision, not a good one but a desperate one, and married Chuck Geisdorf. He had a job on the railroad, a car and a pension. He was the homeliest, most closed off man ever to walk and I am certain you could not have loved him but you needed to survive.

You were cared for and I'm certain he loved you, who wouldn't? You quit drinking and played at a calm, retired life. I grew up and we were a family again.

At the end of your life, saying our goodbyes, you held my hand and said, "We had some good times, didn't we?" and I replied, "Ya Ma, and some real shitty ones, too. I'll forgive you if you forgive me."

Was that the meanest thing a daughter could say, or the most healing? I don't know.

What would I do over? I should have maintained my perfect child patterns and not made things more difficult than they were for both of us. I couldn't undo all the things that made your life so sad. I could have avoided making it worse.

That beautiful woman, ever loving and kind, that came from North Dakota in about 1932, will be the one I hold up for an icon. I am proud to look at those images and claim her as "My Mom."

Ethel - Mom

Licking at life, finding it sweet

40. Herve Kermit Youngdahl Jr.
1937-2013

erm, my loving misfit of a big brother. You were 14 years old when I was born so my earliest recollections of you are around the time you and Lil married. Lil is as much a part of my life and memory as you, and as dear.

Were you ever less than 6'4" tall? Not in my memory. How I miss your voice. "Ya, Pix.."

A natural intellectual in a solidly blue collar world. Dad had imagined his first son to be an athlete and his second to be a scholar. Wrong on both counts.

You had that baby blue eye that flittered around at all times. They call that "lazy eye" but yours looked plenty ambitious, always seeking something to understand. As a small child they thought perhaps you were blind because you didn't seem to follow the lessons in school. You wouldn't count to five in first grade. At age 7, they had you tested to see if perhaps you were retarded. Instead, it seems, your IQ was 137 at that tender age. You likely could have counted for teacher in 4 languages but the suggestion seemed so silly.

You dropped out of high school went into the Airforce and didn't fit there well either. After Dad died, you had a "nervous breakdown" (the details of which are still mysterious) and at the University of MN they did "shock therapy". They did not succeed in closing down your endless stream of consciousness.

So, you wrote. You wrote all the time, everywhere. In coffee shops and bars, at home, on buses. At the end of your life you fought to survive as long as you could put words on paper.

You found Lil, your perfect mate, and moved to Berkeley, CA to go to college. I was still a small kid and California was a world away. You sent me books, Uncle Tom's Cabin, Gulliver's Travels, while I was reading Nancy Drew mysteries. Long distance phone calls were a rare and expensive treat. While you were out there, Lil got pregnant and eventually we were told she had a still born girl. True to our Scandinavian style, it was never again mentioned.

In time you moved back to Minneapolis, ever the student. I believe you attained two Masters degrees and eventually were a Fulbright Scholar teaching at UW Milwaukee. You did not complete your Phd. As you described it, "That degree mill isn't designed for writers with imagination."

My sweetest memories are walking with you to Dinky Town where you would pour through used book stores then take me to dark coffee shops, featuring poets reading to bongo drums. The walks were long for me, you at 6'4" and me about 4' tall, legs frantically trying to keep up. You introduced me to classical music and most priceless, jazz. I love it to this day. I'll hold forever, the image of you singing along with a record of Sarah Vaughn, Lullaby in Birdland.

Your life was simple, yet complex. You had two daughters, Simone and Lisa that you loved dearly.

When you died, I grieved but held fast to the phone conversations we would have, about music, books, politics and movies. Our call always ended, "I love you." "I love you too, kid."

Those words, your voice, live on.

The stone I painted to honor Kerm

Kerm and Pixie

41. Lillian Liefgren Youngdahl
?? 1939-2010

I barely remember Kerm, without you. Perhaps he only existed in your presence. You were more than a sister in law, you were, Kerm and Lil.

Raised on a farm, the oldest of seven kids, with more brains than that small town could hold. You and Kerm met at the U of M and melded into one very unusual being.

You scooped me up, shared your life and all its quirks with me. Poor as you two were, you thrift store and garage sale shopped to create a home. The places you lived were lavishly furnished with books. Books in piles as end tables, books splayed open on table tops and any flat surface. You cooked high end, nontraditional foods on a budget designed for mac and cheese.

Your schizophrenia overtook you sometime in the 60s. No surprise, they call it "Valedictorians Disease". Those years with small kids, in a tiny apartment and your mind creating other images, were hard for the family and I can't guess how they felt to you. I was too young to understand about such diseases and just accepted that, as always, you and Kerm were unusual folks.

In time, you were adequately medicated and the two of you went on to live a quiet, simple life because you had limited tolerance for chaos or change in routines.

You took care of Kerm so faithfully. The night you died, he woke you to make him some peanut butter toast and you fell at his feet when you set the plate before him.

He called me, and we talked on the phone for about two hours that night. He was so lost.

How could life have been had you not found each other? It was an odd, small life full of big thoughts and ideas. Without each other, nah, can't even imagine it.

42. Donald Robert Anderson
January 1, 1942- October 27, 1994

ou were the love of Gege's life from your first blind date when she was fifteen until she drew her last breath in 2016. A tall, handsome brown eyed man from the Northside if Mpls. She thought you must be rich because you had a car and a watch.

I hid behind the door when you came to pick her up that first date, and I giggled like the nine-year-old that I was. I was smitten as well with your good looks.

You married on September 1, 1962. Gege was only seventeen, had dropped out of high school and wished only to be with you. Mom was not happy, as you can imagine. I was an over aged flower girl, too young to be a bridesmaid but Gege kept me at her side for all events.

You went into the service and Gege followed you to Denver, Duluth and Mauston, WI. She'd have followed you into the jungles of South America and you soon learned, I'd have been right behind.

I'm guessing you felt no power to say no, when it came to the repeated chapters of "Pixie is moving in with us for a while." You took us as the inseparable team that we were. One time, in casual conversation about who knows what, you said to Tim, "I thought so too until I married these two!" Yep, it was a twofer…

Over the years you worked as a salesman in a variety of jobs. Gege held the family together through bad times and worse times. She sewed the kids clothes, learned to make the humblest food adequate to nourish all of you. You imagined a life of luxury but sadly, lacked ambition to create it. Gege shared your dreams and was ever your cheerleader.

It was only at the end of your life that you found a job that suited you well, driving bus for MTC. Had you fallen into that twenty years earlier, how much easier it would have been for all of you.

Your loyalty to me, forced or not, was a great gift. You were somehow, one person I could fight with and learn that conflict is not a terminal disease. I'm sure my constant presence was a frustration for you and I thank you for never giving up. At the end of your life I was able to help in small ways, with your care and to hold your hand and say "Thanks, you were a good guy."

To the end, Gege was waiting to be with you. You were never really gone, certainly not from her heart.

You died too young, still handsome and ever Gege's mate. I thank you for loving her enough to allow me as part of the package.

43. Georgiann Youngdahl Anderson
3/30/1945—9/23/2016

ear Geg, How do girls and women survive without a sister? The story is, you dressed up and sat at the curb waiting when Dad picked Mom up from the hospital to bring me home. Since that moment, we clung to each other like Spider Monkeys.

I followed you everywhere. You took me along to every event, made me go to Sunday school, which I hated, brought me along on dates, kept me in your life at all times.

We shared a bed, whispered secrets, but for the six years that separated us, we could have been conjoined. In your presence, I was always safe. Well, except for the accident on the bridge but who knew there was a hole just my size? You never recovered, I could never convince you that I was fine.

That was your nature- to feel bad and guilty for everyone's errors. I often joked, "I don't carry guilt, that's Gege's thing." Nothing in your life deserved your guilt. Ever. Still, you wore it like a coat and it was heavy on your soul.

I always wished to be as smart and as pretty as you. I wanted to do whatever you did. In fact, our styles and paths were very different but you were the person I longed to be.

You got married (much too young, by the way) and poor Don soon learned he signed on for a sister team. He was never rid of me and I know, you'd have shared your home with me, even if it were a tent or a yurt.

Our kids were a collective. Yours, mine, ours, as you said, we raised them like barn cats.

We read each other's minds. Became frustrated with our differences and even fought a time or two. We shared a sharp mind and a quick wit and could finish each other's sentences, or laugh without having to complete the thought.

You never recovered from losing Don. For twenty years you carried on, doing kind things for others, reaching out to rescue your kids and mine. Having grandkids was your respite from grief and you showered them with love and attention.

Your health was never good but failed ever so slowly over the decades without Don. The final straw, after multiple chronic diagnoses, was ovarian cancer. Once again, I am following you.

Right to the end, we shared secrets and the last ones that I squeezed out of you are still safe. Tale telling in the hospice bed, was our perfect goodbye.

I couldn't have wished another day on you just to have you around. We parted ways having shared a perfect love.

I didn't want to start kindergarten but you promised you would look in the window of my classroom every day. I only went based on that promise. You kept it. We shared a lifetime of peeking in each other's windows to offer support. Nothing ever really kept us apart, even your death cannot diminish that connection.

As always, I am right behind you.

44. Phone call

 want to call Gege
To tell her my sister died
No answer
Gege is my sister

I call her
When I'm breaking needles
Trying to finish a quilt

I call her
When the kids are troubled
When the grand kids are adorable
When life is hilarious
When life is frustrating
When fabric is on sale
When I have a crazy dream
When I buy a new purse
Or a car
When I write a bad poem
Or a nearly good one
I always call her if something sad happens

I really need to tell her that
My heart is broken
That my sister died
But Gege is my sister

Gege and her daughters Terri Lynne and Jen

45. Orrin Keith Youngdahl
12/29/41—forever, I hope

T he last one standing in this collection of folks who preceded me. I know that was not your plan but I'm glad that I won't have to bear losing you.

The second son, born in Grandma's house. You were mom's Golden Child. I was never jealous, she was right.

The High Holidays on Monroe St occurred anytime you were home on leave. Her boy was home and all was right with the world.

You and Kerm were so different, hard to believe you came from the same womb and shared dna. Neither of you hung around the house much. Kerm was off reading and writing while you were playing any sport that kept you outdoors. What you shared, was a calm and ever gentle demeanor. Shy as I was about men in general, I was always safe and secure when my brothers were present.

You were the only one of us to graduate from high school. You had a focus and willingness to do the right thing that the rest of us lacked.

It seems the moment you finished, having been trained in aviation mechanics, you joined the Marine Corp. Did you know that would define you? It offered a structure and direction that you needed and served you well.

We all watched the war in Vietnam (the American's War) played out on television news every night. Mom said nothing but she had to have ached inside without rest.

Without question, you were the best looking of the lot. The Hollywood teen of the 50's, slender, perfect hair and those slightly sad blue eyes. Did you drive your cars as much as you worked on them? Cars, cigarettes and a touch of James Dean mystery.

I learned to play the Marine Corp Hymn on that old upright piano in the den to demonstrate my love for you when you came home. You brought me a Marine Corp sweatshirt once and I wore it for years.

In the decades that we were all raising families and living far apart without much contact, did you know you were loved and missed? You were.

Mom, Marie and Agnes, adored and defended their brothers with some ferocity. I believe Gege and I figured out why. Life mates can come and go but brothers are beginning to end.

You should feel proud of the life you lived, the service you offered and for the kind and gentle being that have always been.

Thanks for sharing our crazy history. I think it all turned out just right.

Orrin

Part Three
Promise

It was an amicable parting, me and the Mayo oncologist. He had reviewed the follow-up labs and a recent MRI report. I had read them as well.

He: "Anything I can do for you now will only make you sick and sorry."

Me: "I know. What you have to sell I'm not buying. Tell me what to expect when this thing goes sideways."

He: "Bowel obstruction is always a risk"

Me: "I don't want that. What else?"

He: "Just loss of appetite and sort of wasting away."

Me: "I'll take that one"

He: "Of course, you could get hit by a bus."

Me: "Unlikely where I live."

In three marvelous years since completion of chemo, I grew hair again. Sadly, it was the same limp, unremarkable hair I'd had. For all that, I'd hoped for auburn curls. I felt perfectly fine, the flaw was keeping my follow up schedule so I could reassure them that all was well and leave with a sassy wink and a smile. Now, I left the clinic armed with solid information to the contrary. Cancer gets a double win from me. The data considers a five-year mark as survival. Still, just after that happy day, my death certificate will show cause of death as ovarian cancer. Smooth move, no?

Most of us wish for a sudden death. These are catastrophic for the loved ones left behind but the phrase, "He never knew what hit 'em," is soothing. My gift was that of time. I worked as a triage nurse for much of my career so sorting things out, prioritizing and making lists are my specialty. My health status was non-acute but my life definitely needed a well thought out care plan.

Airway. Breathing. Circulation.

Places. People. Things.

Where had I been? Red push pins on a globe would mark great opportunities. Beaches in Mexico when I still looked presentable in a swim suit. Peru, doing volunteer nursing. Cost a fortune to work harder than I ever have and coming home enriched with a much larger understanding of life on this planet. Africa. While hubby hunted I absorbed a clear sense of how small we are, how new and arrogant in the evolutionary timeline. The recurrence of my cancer was identified just following my fourth trip to Europe. Yes, Paris cafés are all that and more.

All my travel begins in Minneapolis; my heart and soul are designed in that middle size city with big city ways. That is the standard by which I measure any city. Second to Minneapolis, I love Chicago most. Perhaps for the similarities. Chicago is Minneapolis on steroids. Tossing back on a bed in a Chicago hotel, loving the sirens and traffic that soothe me like rain on a roof, walking streets in heat, rain, snow, reading in coffee shops, all lullabies to a soul weary of rural quiet. Imagine, six million people and not one of them needs a thing from me but for the smiles I offer up as payment for letting me share their space.

New York City is constant, pulsing energy. My game there is to smile and say good morning to folks hustling by on the street. They almost pause, uncertain of my intentions then carry on knowing more about the Midwest with a covert cultural anthropology lesson to ponder.

Paris, Rome (which should be called Six Flags over the Vatican). Amsterdam where one can get a contact high from walking past the coffee shops. Austin, Texas, music, food and no cowboy hats. San Francisco, a sea side paradise guaranteed to sculpt those calves climbing hills. Los Angeles, a flat, square parking lot with a pleasant climate but no discernable character. San Diego holds great charm and history. Despite its proximity, it is not a suburb of LA. Phoenix, a hot flat square with too many people and too little water. Las Vegas, everyone should see it once to clarify the definition of ostentatious. Miami looks like a place someone designed with Legos last Wednesday. New Orleans, there is no other city like it in the USA. Food, music and history shimmering in heat and humidity. Washington, DC is what a nation's capital should be. Amazing monuments to our incredible but short history with crushing poverty on the fringes. There is a metaphor in there.

Honolulu is a long way to fly for a crowded beach.

Savannah, a mid-sized city with tremendous pride and charm. I highly recommend the peach cobbler. Beaufort, South Carolina is just as Pat Conroy illustrates in his excellent novels. The Pacific is wild and rugged but that mellow, contemplative southern Atlantic coast has a magical rhythm.

Places I didn't get to but would like to imagine: New England, Portland, Seattle, Boston. Such a short list of regrets is the sign of a fortunate life.

By plane, train or automobile the souvenirs we bring home are intangible. The photos are nice but, trust me, they will bore the snot out of friends and family. "Oh, another shoreline."

Better we capture the feel of a place, talk to a stranger at the next table in a café, ask a local to suggest their favorite corner of town. It's silly to drive a thousand freeway miles to eat supper at Denny's.

I still wake up in the mornings and feel armed to book a flight to Europe but by the time I reached the airport I would need a serious nap. Since my body has grounded me, it's time to sort through stuff.

I'm not a hoarder but one does accrue stuff. I could ignore it and let my family sort it out later but how can they know what matters in a houseful of things that probably don't matter one bit?

The thrift stores have benefitted from clothing and housewares that I probably shouldn't have purchased in the first place. Why leave evidence for my husband of where all his money has gone over forty-four years? I gave away two large crates of record albums, which orchestrate the life of a Baby Boomer. I haven't yet parted with all the 45s. I did a good deal of babysitting to earn the cash for those and every boyfriend from the 60s is named on the labels with little hearts.

Photos. Yikes. During long winters, I have organized and sorted those time and again. Still, there is little order to them and now with all the digital photos my computer is overflowing. I'm trying, really.

My writing is the biggest challenge. The best of it is in journals and there is no rhyme or reason to any of that. I have found some gems that leave me pondering where, why and what was I thinking. I recognize the sloppy handwriting or would wonder who laid that on paper. Sorry kids, you can figure that out.

Novelty baubles and jewelry that I picked up while traveling or as a mood-altering behavior. When I worked it was fun to disguise a plain wardrobe with a funky necklace or a hunk of sterling on my wrist. On Thanksgiving when all the girls were here I hauled it all out and let them grab as if it were pirates treasure. None of it was of any monetary value but small reminders of a trip to Chicago or New York. The few pieces of "real" stuff I took to my favorite goldsmith (who had designed most of it), had it cleaned and repackaged to hand off to my daughter and granddaughters. None of it is worthy of a jewel safe or a family feud but might add a little twinkle to my lovely girls, or something to pawn if they come upon hard times.

Any fool knows at the end of the journey, that stuff is just stuff. Thrift stores and garage sales illustrate the trivial meaning of all that. Still, picking up pebbles and shells on a beach reminds us of a moment in the sun.

I've approached this process as if I'm moving out of the joint. I guess I am.

People are the greatest gift in any life, certainly in mine. How does one begin to sort the smiles and voices that fill a life? Back in the days when people were serious about sending Christmas cards I knew a woman who kept a separate address book for that task. It featured a column for checking off if a card was received and if she didn't get one, next year, she didn't send one. If relationships could be so simple. Family is a collective of folks we don't choose but do get attached to. We can feel as much fondness for a cousin we rarely see as we do for a sister in law who is ever present. It's perfectly okay to have favorites and make choices about the company we prefer. How many movies have been made about family gatherings for holidays and funerals? Those gatherings are a practice in playground politics with an open bar. Something about the ritual is comforting, waiting for the cordiality to shift to subtle insults, the gossip in the kitchen, the uncle whose voice keeps rising as he tells the same stories again and again, kids running amok, eyes rolling because someone really brought a store-bought pie. Throw a brand-new second spouse into the mix or better yet, a pregnant teen and everyone takes away enough warmth, joy and laughter to last a year. Rewind, do it again, and again. If no gun play is involved, it's a success.

Mostly, we do choose who in the family we most enjoy. Those are the ones to seek out, hold onto and sort with the group called friends.

I know lots of women without husbands or children who live perfectly full lives. To be a woman without girlfriends, to me, would be walking a desert with only potato chips at hand. Sociologists have shown repeatedly, that women are at the core of family relationships. If women can hold together a loose collection of ages, genders and proclivities, how masterful must we be at holding one another? Girlfriends in elementary school while the boys are eating dirt and boogers; in adolescence when your body is horrifying; as a young adult walking through every drama; marriages, raising kids, working a job and making sure every member of the household is tended to, divorce, kids in trouble, illness, injury, all of it is palatable when girlfriends gather up to laugh. Men have friends to share activities and certainly they care about one another but they would probably live longer if they could learn to giggle until they wet their pants. That may well be the secret to female longevity.

I call my men friends my Decoy Boys. Let my husband wonder if one among 'em is special. Truly, the men in my life enrich me, and I could never live in a marriage that did not allow them. Doctors, lawyers, writers, writers, writers and a felon here and there, all bring a masculine perspective to my life and appear sincerely interested in my world view. It seems unlikely that it's my smokin' hot bod because they bring no bouquets or candy but have filled my life with brilliant conversation and humor. Feel free to start rumors, it can only enhance my image at this point.

Since I am suffering diminished energy I am being selective about social engagement. I love good conversation, it is my drug of choice. I can't spend any time now on empty activity. No more baby showers, wedding showers or Tupperware parties for me. I promise.

Things and places help define us but it's the people, past and present that make sense of it all.

My family, their names are not necessary because all that will be in an obituary. Those funny, loyal, smart people who circle the wagons in difficult times. I will confess that my greatest challenge with this miserable illness, which is not going to concede defeat, is the sadness in their eyes. It's my job to fix things, make their paths easier when I can, walk them through their painful times. Now, here I am, the source of all that with no reassurances to offer. The moments I should be here for, I won't. The pain of this disease is managed chemically but I can't fix the tears they shed when we hug. Best that the grandkids learn about grief in this perfectly natural way; but shouldn't mine be the lap they seek?

My lesson must be, "Let it go, you're not All Powerful"

Everyone in my life can know, if I ever said, "I love you," they can hold that to be true. Promise.

Photos

Uncle Jim Eide

Grandpa Alfred Youngdahl (Youngdale)

Grandpa Alfred with a friend

Marie Youngdahl

Gege

With Gege at book signing

Orrin and Gege

Jason and Orrin

Lost Lake Folk Art
SHIPWRECKT BOOKS PUBLISHING COMPANY

www.ingramcontent.com/pod-product-compliance
Lightning Source LLC
Chambersburg PA
CBHW071127090426
42736CB00012B/2040